Alice's Cook Book

a culinary diversion

Alice's
Cook Book

a culinary diversion

John Fisher

with illustrations by
Sir John Tenniel

FREDERICK MULLER LIMITED

First published in Great Britain 1975 by
Frederick Muller Limited, London NW2 6LE

Phototypeset by Tradespools Ltd, Frome, Somerset
Printed and bound by A. Wheaton & Company, Exeter
ISBN: 0 584 10405 7

For Hannah

Contents

Introduction

That the Alice who by courtesy of Lewis Carroll's imagination threaded her way apprehensively through Wonderland and then melted mistily through the Looking-Glass should find her name attached to a cook book, should surprise no one familiar with the actual books which chronicled her adventures. As the following pages will show, references to food and eating abound in Carroll's two masterpieces with the frequency of currants in a Victorian Christmas pudding. No sooner has Alice entered the rabbit-hole than she is clutching a jar labelled "Orange Marmalade". She has scarcely had time to gather her thoughts before she is pondering the now proverbial questions, "Do cats eat bats?" and "Do bats eat cats?". The jar proves empty, Alice comes to realise that the problem of feeding Dinah, her cat, is now out of her control, and the tone is set for the continuing motif.

It is a tone of tension and frustration. Whenever Alice herself does come to eat or drink, her efforts are either at the last moment thwarted or she undergoes some traumatic change in her physical condition as a gastronomic after-effect, a change quite inconceivable in our own world outside a fairground Hall of Mirrors. "Drink Me" and "Eat Me" soon become invitations to extreme and conflicting changes in size. The Mad Hatter's Tea Party becomes the most tedious of lost causes: she gets nothing to eat at all. The plum-cake of the Lion and the Unicorn not only proves impossible to cut, but when it divides itself into slices makes no provision for the puzzled Alice. At the Looking-Glass banquet, Alice misses the soup and fish, etiquette prevents her partaking of the mutton, and the bottles, in imaginative liaison with the plates, assume wings. In the court episodes, food, in the form of stolen jam tarts and onions mistaken for tulip bulbs, becomes a source of guilt as well as discomfort. The oyster poem of the Walrus and the Carpenter and the soup episode of Pig and Pepper reverberate with cruelty.

Critics and psychoanalysts have long read into such references a lingering obsession on Carroll's part with the rivalry bound to colour a childhood shared with no less than three brothers and seven sisters, a rivalry doubtless expressed at that early age, as in the books, in terms of food fads and favouritism. Such theories lose no ground from the fact that the gastronomic motif informs some of the earliest work attributable to Carroll. One poem, "Brother and Sister", written as early as 1845 (Carroll, or Charles Lutwidge Dodgson, to give him his real name, was born on January 27th, 1832 and died on January 14th, 1898), after reporting the failure of a brother to borrow a frying pan from the cook to make mutton broth out of his sibling, ends with the moral, "Never stew your sister". Eight years later in *Mischmasch*, one of the magazines written and edited by Carroll for the amusement of his family, he published "The Two Brothers", a poem in which the older uses the younger as bait on a fish-hook:

> *The fish hurried up by the dozens,*
> *All ready and eager to bite,*
> *For the lad that he flung was so tender and young,*
> *It quite gave them an appetite.*

In turn their sister's heart "brake into three" and we hear her lament

> —, *"One of the two will be wet through and through,*
> *and t'other'll be late for tea!"*

Phyllis Greenacre, one of the leading proponents of this school of criticism, has also drawn attention to an early drawing by Carroll entitled "The Scanty Meal", which appeared in *The Rectory Umbrella*, another household magazine. Intended at once as a parody of an existing picture by J. F. Herring and as an illustration of "the evils of homoeopathy (the science of taking medicine in infinitely small doses)", it depicts grimly a Spartan family dinner table watched over by a butler who confesses that "only a billionth of an ounce of bread" is left and that the cook "must keep that for next week!",

10

whereupon mother demands that "a trillionth more" should be ordered from the baker. Meanwhile, the speech-bubble comment by an elder brother, "I'm afraid there's more than half a particle of beer here. If so, I daren't drink it", suggests Carroll's own abstemiousness; while the wasp-waisted thinness of all present recalls his continued practice, as an artist, most evident in his own drawings for the first version of "Alice's Adventures in Wonderland", of drawing thin people abnormally thin and fat people abnormally fat. Most relevant to the rivalry theme is the complaint regarding her sister of one small girl to her mother: "Ma! *ought* Sophy to have another molecule? I saw the last she had distinctly!"

To many the interpretation of sibling rivalry will appear too ingenious. There is no reason why Alice's difficulties with food and drink should be anything more than a fantastical exaggeration of the experiences of every child, with or without brothers and sisters, who has ever been fobbed off with traditional nonsense phrases like "Fresh air and snowballs" or—more abruptly—"Nowt—warmed up", when he persists in asking his mother: "What's for dinner?"; who has ever had titbits confiscated for eating between meals; who has ever had it drummed into him that, in a world where children are meant to be seen and not heard, nowhere is that more rigidly expected than at table, that domestic shrine of good manners.

What is beyond dispute, however, is Carroll's continued use throughout his literary career of the theme of eating and, especially, the obstacles placed in the path of appetite. The mysterious title-creature of his famous nonsense poem, "The Hunting of the Snark" (1876), could be said to symbolise food. At least the first of "the five unmistakable marks" detailed by the Bellman for easy identification of the elusive creature is its taste,

> *"Which is meagre and hollow, but crisp:*
> *Like a coat that is rather too tight in the waist,*
> *With a flavour of Will-o'-the-wisp."*

It is worth noting that the Bellman shares his voyage of exploration with a Butcher who can only slaughter beavers and a Baker no less restricted in that he can only bake wedding cake, "for which . . . no materials were to be had". When the Snark is at last "found", he happens to be of the Boojum variety. If you set eyes upon a Boojum you disappear in an instant, exactly the fate

11

that befalls the Baker at the poem's end.

The last of Carroll's writings to appear in print during his lifetime was no less than an introduction to E. G. Wilcox's aptly named children's story, *The Lost Plum Cake* (1897).

Ten years later came the first publication of "Feeding The Mind", a lecture originally delivered in October 1884 and included in this book as an appendix, in which Carroll advocates that the care we take in nourishing the body should be more readily applied in the case of the mind; where, for example, an excess of sugar-plums will as inevitably lead to an attack of indigestion for which now a dreaded dose of "the plainest reading" is the only cure. The piece is entertaining at two levels, both for its subtle whimsy and for the insight it provides into the author's own eating habits, in a way that the zany asides on the subject in letters to his young friends—poised, as they are, on a thin line between fact and fantasy—don't really do. On January 22nd, 1878, for example, he wrote to Jessie Sinclair:

> "I may as well just tell you a few of the things
> I like, and then, whenever you want to give
> me a birthday present (my birthday comes
> once every seven years, on the fifth Tuesday
> in April) you will know what to give me.
> Well, I like *very* much indeed, a little mustard
> with a bit of beef spread thinly under it; and I
> like brown sugar—only it should have some
> apple pudding mixed up with it to keep it
> from being too sweet; but perhaps what I like
> best of all is salt, with some soup poured over
> it. The use of the soup is to hinder the salt from
> being too dry; and it helps to melt it."

One will never know whether this should be treated any more seriously than his suggestion in another letter that the abbreviation R.S.V.P. at the foot of an invitation stands for the dress that must be worn at such functions: "Red Scarf: Vest, Pink".

In keeping with the self-discipline of his life as lecturer and tutor in mathematics at Christ Church College, Oxford, he was abstemious to a

12

fault. His regular lunch, even when a guest at the houses of other people, never exceeded a glass of sherry and a dry biscuit, much to the bewilderment of his young friends whose excessively healthy appetites astonished, even horrified him in turn. In his recognition of eating as a social activity as well as an essential biological function he did nothing if not call the tune. Away from the safe confines of his own quarters in Tom Quad, Christ Church high table, and the Senior Common Room, he generally disliked dinner-parties—"bandying small talk with dull people"—which may be a comment on his own shyness and stammer as much as upon the company he would have to keep. He did, in fact, make a rule of never accepting invitations, to which he objected as an intrusion in their own right. His standard reply recalls Groucho Marx declining membership of a select Hollywood club on the grounds that he did not care to belong to any social organisation that would accept him as a member: "Because you have invited me, therefore I cannot come." This did not, however, prevent him from sending out invitations of his own. He wrote in "Sylvie and Bruno Concluded" (1893): "The great advantage of dinner-parties is that it helps you to see your friends. If you want to *see* a man, offer him something to eat. The same rule with a mouse." Carroll made sure he did most of the offering.

He performed his duties as a host with the almost military precision with which he conducted all aspects of his daily routine, with the exception of his hour of retiring which varied with the amount of work still left undone at nightfall. His diaries reveal how the seating arrangements for each party were assiduously recorded. He kept a menu register so that the same guests would not be served the same dish too often.

The latter system was not foolproof. His favourite form of entertaining was *dîner à deux*, his favourite guests his young girl friends. It is in their reminiscences that we find the flesh of description demanded by the bare bones of his own records. Edith Olivier, in her book *Without Knowing Mr. Walkley*, writes of a typical Dodgson dinner:

> "His position in Oxford was such that in his case alone our rigid rule of chaperonage was waived. If our authorities were sticklers for chaperons, he was equally a stickler for none. 'I only like a *tête-à-tête* dinner,' he said. 'And if you don't come alone, you shan't come at

all'. . . . The food was always the same. Only
two courses—first, some well-cooked mutton
chops, and then, meringues. A glass or two of
port followed, and, an hour after dinner, we
had tea."

Another friend, Isa Bowman, in her own *Story of Lewis Carroll*, has
described his special method for making the tea:

"He was very particular about his tea, which
he always made himself, and in order that it
should draw properly he would walk about
the room swinging the tea-pot from side to
side for exactly ten minutes. The idea of the
grave professor promenading his book-lined
study and carefully waving a tea-pot to and
fro may seem ridiculous, but all the minutiae
of life received an extreme attention at his
hands, and after the first surprise one came
quickly to realise the convenience that his
carefulness ensured."

In later life another eccentric detail added itself to the ritual. His White
Knight's mind devised a special attachment, like a saucepan handle, with
which he could lift the kettle off the fire and pour without burning his hands
or having to find a dirty kettle-holder which invariably got lost.

Other sources of fascination for his young guests included dressing up to
be photographed by him in the messy days long before dry-plates were
invented; games, tricks and puzzles of which he was a fertile inventor;
musical boxes that he would play backwards; automata like a bear that
walked and a bat that flew. In the *Cornhill Magazine* for July 1932, however,
Alice Liddell, the inspiration for the original Alice, left one in no doubt
where the real highlight of a visit lay, namely in his story-telling:

"We used to sit on the big sofa on each side of
him while he told us stories, illustrating them
by pencil or ink drawings as he went along. . . .
He seemed to have an endless store of these
fantastical tales, which he made up as he told

14

them, drawing busily on a large sheet of paper all the time."

But Alice's own opportunities for breaking bread with Carroll were not confined to his rooms:

> "When we went on the river for the afternoon with Mr. Dodgson, which happened at most four or five times every summer term, he always brought with him a large basket full of cakes, and a kettle, which we used to boil under a haycock, if we could find one. On rarer occasions we went out for the whole day with him, and then we took a large basket with luncheon—cold chicken and salad and all sorts of good things."

On just such a picnic, on July 4th, 1862, "Alice's Adventures in Wonderland" were told for the first time.

It is the purpose of the book that follows to provide a practical blueprint for readers of all ages who wish to take their own vicarious experience of those adventures one dimension beyond that of the printed page, to a world not too far beyond Carroll's own imagination, where it is feasible that crusts really do make your hair curl and rabbits—white, of course—really do testify to the ophthalmic virtues of orange root vegetables.

' 'Twas brillig'

"You seem very clever at explaining words, Sir," said Alice. "Would you kindly tell me the meaning of the poem called 'Jabberwocky'?"

"Let's hear it," said Humpty Dumpty. "I can explain all the poems that ever were invented—and a good many that haven't been invented just yet."

This sounded very hopeful, so Alice repeated the first verse:—

> " 'Twas brillig, and the slithy toves
>   Did gyre and gimble in the wabe:
> All mimsy were the borogoves,
>   And the mome raths outgrabe."

"That's enough to begin with," Humpty Dumpty interrupted: "there are plenty of hard words there. *Brillig* means four o'clock in the afternoon— the time when you begin *broiling* things for dinner."

"That'll do very well," said Alice.

THROUGH THE LOOKING-GLASS

But first some simple points regarding the recipes:

1 All spoonfuls are level, unless otherwise stated.

2 All flour is plain, unless self-raising is specified.

3 In pre-heating an oven, allow about 15 minutes.

4 It is hard to assess quantities catered for because appetites vary so much—but always a dish will provide ample for at least 4 people, unless the recipe states otherwise, obviously represents an individual portion, or is a bulk exercise like making jam or marmalade.

5 Finally, should you find yourself having to work in metric, remember that 1 pint equals 568 millilitres, while 1 ounce is the equivalent of 28·35 grammes —commonly calculated at 30 grammes, with 4 ounces, 8 ounces and 1 pound given at 115, 225 and 455 grammes respectively. British pints are used throughout, and 1 US pint is equal to $\frac{3}{5}$ of a British pint.

Lewis Carroll's
Oxford Marmalade

The rabbit-hole went straight on like a tunnel for some way, and then dipped suddenly down, so suddenly that Alice had not a moment to think about stopping herself before she found herself falling down what seemed to be a very deep well.

Either the well was very deep, or she fell very slowly, for she had plenty of time as she went down to look about her, and to wonder what was going to happen next. First, she tried to look down and make out what she was coming to, but it was too dark to see anything: then she looked at the sides of the well, and noticed that they were filled with cupboards and book-shelves: here and there she saw maps and pictures hung upon pegs. She took down a jar from one of the shelves as she passed: it was labelled "ORANGE MARMALADE," but to her great disappointment it was empty: she did not like to drop the jar, for fear of killing somebody underneath, so managed to put it into one of the cupboards as she fell past it.

"Well!" thought Alice to herself, "after such a fall as this, I shall think nothing of tumbling down stairs! How brave they'll all think me at home! Why, I wouldn't say anything about it, even if I fell off the top of the house!" (which was very likely true.)

ALICE'S ADVENTURES IN WONDERLAND

2 pounds Seville oranges / 2 small lemons / 6 pints water / 6 pounds granulated sugar / 1 teaspoon salt / ½ ounce black treacle

1 Wash the oranges and lemons and cut them in half.

2 Squeeze out their juice, discarding the pips and any excess pith or membrane.

3 Slice the peel with a sharp knife to the desired thickness, whether wispy thin or chunky thick.

4 Put peel and juice into a large pan, pour on water, and leave to stand overnight.

5 The following morning, boil gently until the rind is tender and the liquid has reduced by about a third, approximate time 1½ to 2 hours.

6 Add salt, sugar and treacle, stirring well until dissolved.

7 Step up the heat, boiling briskly until the mixture jells. To test that it has, put a little marmalade on a cold plate. Leave a few moments, then touch the blob with your finger. If the surface wrinkles, setting point has been reached.

8 These measurements will produce about 10 pounds of marmalade. Have an appropriate number of jars at hand. They should be warm. Pot the mixture accordingly with a ladle or a small jug.

9 With the marmalade still hot, place a waxed paper disc on each top, smoothing down to eliminate bubbles.

10 Leave all to cool, and don't eat until another day.

11 Keep out of the hands of White Rabbits.

'Drink Me'
Soup

There seemed to be no use in waiting by the little door, so she went back to the table, half hoping she might find another key on it, or at any rate a book of rules for shutting people up like telescopes: this time she found a little bottle on it, ("which certainly was not here before," said Alice,) and round the neck of the bottle was a paper label with the words "DRINK ME" beautifully printed on it in large letters.

It was all very well to say "Drink me," but the wise little Alice was not going to do *that* in a hurry. "No, I'll look first," she said, "and see whether it's marked '*poison*' or not": for she had read several nice little stories about

children who had got burnt, and eaten up by wild beasts, and other unpleasant things, all because they *would* not remember the simple rules their
friends had taught them: such as, that a rod-hot poker will burn you if you
hold it too long; and that, if you cut your finger *very* deeply with a knife, it
usually bleeds; and she had never forgotten that, if you drink much from a
bottle marked "poison," it is almost certain to disagree with you, sooner or
later.

However, this bottle was *not* marked "poison," so Alice ventured to
taste it, and, finding it very nice (it had, in fact, a sort of mixed flavour of
cherry-tart, custard, pine-apple, roast turkey, toffy, and hot buttered toast),
she very soon finished it off.

★   ★   ★   ★   ★

"What a curious feeling!" said Alice, "I must be shutting up like a
telescope!"

ALICE'S ADVENTURES IN WONDERLAND

---

*1 orange / 1 lemon / 1 pear / 1 apple / any other fruit in season, within
reason, such as pineapple or tart-cherries / ½ pound soft brown sugar /
2 tablespoons cornflour / 2 pints water or, preferably, fruit stock / ratafia
biscuits (in lieu of "hot buttered toast")*

1 Wash, peel, and stone all the fruit, cutting into small pieces, with the exception of the lemon.

2 Put the pieces into the stock and simmer until soft.

3 Squeeze the lemon and add its juice to the pan. Also the sugar and the grated lemon rind for zest.

4 Bring mixture to the boil.

5 Having mixed cornflour with 2 tablespoons of cold water, add this to the seething soup, stirring all the time.

6 Boil for 5 more minutes, even longer if the taste of the cornflour persists.

7 Serve chilled with ratafia biscuits.

8 Eat slowly to prevent shrinking fast.

'Eat Me' Cakes

Soon her eye fell on a little glass box that was lying under the table: she opened it, and found in it a very small cake, on which the words "EAT ME" were beautifully marked in currants. "Well, I'll eat it," said Alice, "and if it makes me grow larger, I can reach the key; and if it makes me grow smaller, I can creep under the door: so either way I'll get into the garden, and I don't care which happens!"

She ate a little bit, and said anxiously to herself "Which way? Which way?" holding her hand on the top of her head to feel which way it was growing; and she was quite surprised to find that she remained the same size. To be sure, this is what generally happens when one eats cake; but Alice had got so much into the way of expecting nothing but out-of-the-way things to happen, that it seemed quite dull and stupid for life to go on in the common way.

So she set to work, and very soon finished off the cake.

★   ★   ★   ★   ★

"Curiouser and curiouser!" cried Alice (she was so much surprised, that for the moment she quite forgot how to speak good English). "Now I'm opening out like the largest telescope that ever was! Goodbye, feet!" (for when she looked down at her feet, they seemed to be almost out of sight, they were getting so far off). "Oh, my poor little feet, I wonder who will put on your shoes and stockings for you now, dears? I'm sure *I* shan't be able! I shall be a great deal too far off to trouble myself about you: you must manage the best way you can—but I must be kind to them," thought Alice, "or perhaps they won't walk the way I want to go! Let me see. I'll give them a new pair of boots every Christmas."

ALICE'S ADVENTURES IN WONDERLAND

---

6 ounces cocoa / 6 ounces ground almonds / 6 ounces butter / 6 ounces sugar / 6 ounces Petit Beurre biscuits / 1 egg / 1 extra yolk / currants, maybe

1 To make this most concentrated of confections, the cake guaranteed to fill you, to stretch you more than any other, first knead the butter and cocoa together into a smooth paste.

2 Work in the ground almonds.

3 After melting the sugar in a few drops of water over a slight flame, stir this into the mixture.

4 Also the eggs.

5 Break the biscuits gently into small pebble-sized nuggets.

6 Stir in all but a few of the pieces.

7 Divide the mixture into individual paper cake cases, the insides of which have been rubbed with sweet almond oil.

8 With the remaining pieces of biscuit or with currants, spell out "EAT ME" on top of the one **you** will eat.

9 To "cook", store in a refrigerator for a day.

10 Watch your head on the ceiling.

Caucus Comfits

"What *is* a Caucus-race?" said Alice; not that she much wanted to know, but the Dodo had paused as if it thought that *somebody* ought to speak, and no one else seemed inclined to say anything.

"Why," said the Dodo, "the best way to explain it is to do it." (And, as you might like to try the thing yourself, some winter day, I will tell you how the Dodo managed it.)

First it marked out a race-course, in a sort of circle, ("the exact shape doesn't matter," it said,) and then all the party were placed along the course, here and there. There was no "One, two, three, and away!" but they began running when they liked, and left off when they liked, so that it was not easy to know when the race was over. However, when they had been running half-an-hour or so, and were quite dry again, the Dodo suddenly called out, "The race is over!" and they all crowded round it, panting, and asking, "But who has won?"

This question the Dodo could not answer without a great deal of thought, and it stood for a long time with one finger pressed upon its forehead, (the position in which you usually see Shakespeare, in the pictures of him,) while the rest waited in silence. At last the Dodo said "*Everybody* has won, and *all* must have prizes."

"But who is to give the prizes?" quite a chorus of voices asked.

"Why, *she*, of course," said the Dodo, pointing to Alice with one finger; and the whole party at once crowded round her, calling out, in a confused way, "Prizes! Prizes!"

Alice had no idea what to do, and in despair she put her hand in her pocket, and pulled out a box of comfits (luckily the salt water had not got into it), and handed them round as prizes. There was exacly one a-piece, all round.

ALICE'S ADVENTURES IN WONDERLAND

orange segments / pineapple segments / grapes / cherries / one-eighth pint water / 4 ounces sugar / pinch of cream of tartar / a candy thermometer

1 Pour water into saucepan over a low heat.

2 Stir in the sugar until it is completely dissolved.

3 Add the cream of tartar dissolved in a few drops of water.

4 Boil quickly to 290° Fahrenheit.

5 Without delay take saucepan away from the heat.

6 When the bubbles have subsided, dip each fruit or piece of fruit (needless to say, stoned, peeled, and dry) into the syrup, using a pickle-fork or the end of a metal knitting needle or whatever.

7 Transfer the fruit, thoroughly coated, to a sheet of oiled or greaseproof paper.

8 Leave until set and the comfit boasts a transparent sheen.

9 When the syrup has dried, you may, should you please, brush each comfit with egg white and then dust with fine castor sugar to obtain a frosted effect.

10 Store in an air-tight jar or tin, well away from salt water.

Pebble Cakes

"We must burn the house down!" said the Rabbit's voice, and Alice called out as loud as she could, "If you do, I'll set Dinah at you!"

There was a dead silence instantly, and Alice thought to herself, "I wonder what they *will* do next! If they had any sense, they'd take the roof off." After a minute or two, they began moving about again, and Alice heard the Rabbit say, "A barrowful will do, to begin with."

"A barrowful of *what*?" thought Alice. But she had not long to doubt, for the next moment a shower of little pebbles came rattling in at the window, and some of them hit her in the face. "I'll put a stop to his," she said to herself and shouted out, "You'd better not do that again!" which produced another dead silence.

Alice noticed, with some surprise, that the pebbles were all turning into little cakes as they lay on the floor, and a bright idea came into her head. "If I eat one of these cakes," she thought, "it's sure to make some change in my size; and, as it can't possibly make me larger, it must make me smaller, I suppose."

So she swallowed one of the cakes, and was delighted to find that she began shrinking directly. As soon as she was small enough to get through the door, she ran out of the house, and found quite a crowd of little animals and birds waiting outside.

ALICE'S ADVENTURES IN WONDERLAND

---

8 ounces self-raising flour | 3 ounces sugar | 1 ounce chopped candied peel | 1 egg | 2 ounces currants | 4 ounces butter or margarine | 1 pinch of salt | 1 pinch of nutmeg | 1 pinch of mixed spice

1 Sieve the flour into a mixing bowl.

2 Throw in salt, nutmeg, and spice.

3 Chop up butter and rub it into the flour with the fingers until it resembles fine breadcrumbs.

4 Add currants, peel, and sugar.

5 Beat egg in a separate basin with a fork, and add to the other ingredients.

6 Mix everything together, adding just a drop of milk if things appear *too* dry.

7 Grease a baking tin and pile the mixture upon it in small rough-looking heaps.

8 Bake for 15 minutes in a moderately hot oven at about 400 degrees Fahrenheit, Gas Mark 6.

9 Then find a house that fits.

Ambidextrous Mushrooms

This time Alice waited patiently until it chose to speak again. In a minute or two the Caterpillar took the hookah out of its mouth, and yawned once or twice, and shook itself. Then it got down off the mushroom, and crawled away into the grass, merely remarking, as it went, "One side will make you grow taller, and the other side will make you grow shorter."

"One side of *what*? The other side of *what*?" thought Alice to herself.

"Of the mushroom," said the Caterpillar, just as if she had asked it aloud; and in another moment it was out of sight.

Alice remained looking thoughtfully at the mushroom for a minute, trying to make out which were the two sides of it; and, as it was perfectly round, she found this a very difficult question. However, at last she stretched her arms round it as far as they would go, and broke off a bit of the edge with each hand.

"And now which is which?" she said to herself, and nibbled a little of the right-hand bit to try the effect. The next moment she felt a violent blow underneath her chin: it had struck her foot!

ALICE'S ADVENTURES IN WONDERLAND

1 pound mushrooms / 8 fluid ounces sour cream / 2 teaspoons flour / 2 ounces butter / 1 small chopped onion / salt / pepper / lemon juice

1 Wash and dry the mushrooms, keeping the stalks intact.

2 Slice them, stalks included.

3 Melt the butter in a frying pan.

4 Add onion and mushrooms, and fry for five minutes.

5 Stir in the flour and salt and pepper to taste.

6 After a few minutes, stir in the sour cream, without letting the mixture come to the boil.

7 Add lemon juice, again according to taste.

8 Serve on rounds of hot buttered toast.

9 Choose the right or left side and nibble cautiously.

Eggs Bonne Alice

"But I'm *not* a serpent, I tell you!" said Alice. "I'm a—I'm a—"

"Well. *What* are you?" said the Pigeon. "I can see you're trying to invent something!"

"I—I'm a little girl," said Alice, rather doubtfully, as she remembered the number of changes she had gone through, that day.

"A likely story indeed!" said the Pigeon in a tone of the deepest contempt. "I've seen a good many little girls in my time, but never *one* with such a neck as that! No, no! You're a serpent; and there's no use denying it. I suppose you'll be telling me next that you never tasted an egg!"

"I *have* tasted eggs, certainly," said Alice, who was a very truthful child; "but little girls eat eggs quite as much as serpents do, you know."

"I don't believe it," said the Pigeon; "but if they do, why, then they're a kind of serpent: that's all I can say."

This was such a new idea to Alice, that she was quite silent for a minute or two, which gave the Pigeon the opportunity of adding, "You're looking for eggs, I know *that* well enough; and what does it matter to me whether you're a little girl or a serpent?"

"It matters a good deal to *me*," said Alice hastily; "but I'm not looking for eggs, as it happens; and, if I was, I shouldn't want *yours*: I don't like them raw."

ALICE'S ADVENTURES IN WONDERLAND

1 egg / 1 tablespoon spinach purée / 1 tablespoon single cream / butter / cheese / pepper / individual small baking dishes or cocottes for each portion (ingredients given for individual portion)

1 Grease the container heavily with butter.

2 Break egg straight into container.

3 Add spinach to cover the egg.

4 Sprinkle with pepper and grated cheese.

5 Add cream.

6 Stand the dish in a pan containing hot, near to boiling, water that comes half-way up the side of the dish.

7 Cover pan with lid or cooking foil.

8 Bake in a moderate oven for not more than eight minutes at 350 degrees Fahrenheit, Gas Mark 4, until egg is *just* set.

9 Eat straight from the individual cocotte as soon as cooking time is up, else the heat contained in the dish will go on cooking the egg.

10 Why spinach? Serpents don't eat spinach, that's why!

Not
'Too Much Pepper'
Soup

The door led right into a large kitchen, which was full of smoke from one end to the other: the Duchess was sitting on a three-legged stool in the middle, nursing a baby: the cook was leaning over the fire, stirring a large cauldron which seemed to be full of soup.

34

"There's certainly too much pepper in that soup!" Alice said to herself, as well as she could for sneezing.

There was certainly too much of it in the *air*. Even the Duchess sneezed occasionally; and as for the baby, it was sneezing and howling alternately without a moment's pause. The only two creatures in the kitchen, that did *not* sneeze, were the cook, and a large cat, which was lying on the hearth and grinning from ear to ear.

ALICE'S ADVENTURES IN WONDERLAND

1¼ pounds potatoes, peeled and quartered / 2 bunches chopped watercress, as a hot pepper substitute / freshly ground pepper, the genuine thing / 3 large chopped onions / 3 pints white stock or, failing that, salted water / 1 gill double cream / salt

1 Boil potatoes and onions in stock until thoroughly cooked.

2 Rub them through a sieve, returning the purée to the stock.

3 Bring mixture to the boil.

4 Add chopped watercress and boil for 15 minutes.

5 Season with *plenty* of freshly ground pepper, but not *"too much"*.

6 Also salt to taste.

7 If you want to serve the soup hot, stir in the cream gently.

8 If cold, chill and stir in the cream just before serving.

9 Garnish with chopped watercress.

10 And remember, table napkins are not for sneezing into.

"Oh, don't bother *me*," said the Duchess. "I never could abide figures!" And with that she began nursing her child again, singing a sort of lullaby to it as she did so, and giving it a violent shake at the end of every line:

"Speak roughly to your little boy,
  And beat him when he sneezes:
He only does it to annoy,
  Because he knows it teases."

CHORUS

(in which the cook and the baby joined):—

"Wow! wow! wow!"

While the Duchess sang the second verse of the song, she kept tossing the baby violently up and down, and the poor little thing howled so, that Alice could hardly hear the words:

"I speak severely to my boy,
  And beat him when he sneezes:
For he can thoroughly enjoy
  The pepper when he pleases!"

"Wow! wow! wow!"

The Cheshire Cat's Cheese Whiskers

"Please would you tell me," said Alice, a little timidly, for she was not quite sure whether it was good manners for her to speak first, "why your cat grins like that?"

"It's a Cheshire cat," said the Duchess, "and that's why. Pig!"

She said the last word with such sudden violence that Alice quite jumped; but she saw in another moment that it was addressed to the baby, and not to her, so she took courage, and went on again:—

"I didn't know that Cheshire cats always grinned; in fact, I didn't know that cats *could* grin."

"They all can," said the Duchess; "and most of 'em do."

"I don't know of any that do," Alice said very politely, feeling quite pleased to have got into a conversation.

"You don't know much," said the Duchess; "and that's a fact."

ALICE'S ADVENTURES IN WONDERLAND

---

2 ounces flour / 2 ounces butter / 3 ounces grated Cheddar cheese / ½ teaspoon baking powder / 2 ounces grated breadcrumbs / ½ saltspoon salt / ½ saltspoon pepper / paprika

1 Sieve flour, salt and pepper into a basin.

2 Stir in the breadcrumbs and cheese.

3 Rub in the butter with the fingers until you get a smooth paste, adding a little milk if the texture proves difficult.

37

4 Dust working surface with flour and roll out pastry into a strip about 4 inches wide, one-eighth of an inch thick.

5 Cut pastry into so many thin strips.

6 Place on a greased tin and bake in a steady oven at 375 degrees Fahrenheit, Gas Mark 4, until crisp and brown.

7 Serve hot, sprinkled with paprika.

8 Then sit back and smile contentedly at your achievement, if only to remind yourself that long ago Cheshire Cheeses were moulded into the shape of a grinning cat prior to being sent to Bristol for export. Hence, maybe, the origin of the phrase "grin like a Cheshire cat". Perhaps Alice should have asked her question of the Duchess's cook?

The Mad Hatter's Doughnuts

"Your hair wants cutting," said the Hatter. He had been looking at Alice for some time with great curiosity, and this was his first speech.

"You should learn not to make personal remarks," Alice said with some severity: "It's very rude."

The Hatter opened his eyes very wide on hearing this; but all he *said* was, "Why is a raven like a writing-desk?"

"Come, we shall have some fun now!" thought Alice. "I'm glad they've begun asking riddles—I believe I can guess that," she added aloud.

"Do you mean that you think you can find out the answer to it?" said the March Hare.

"Exactly so," said Alice.

"Then you should say what you mean," the March Hare went on.

"I do," Alice hastily replied; "at least—at least I mean what I say—that's the same thing, you know."

"Not the same thing a bit!" said the Hatter. "Why, you might just as well say that 'I see what I eat' is the same thing as 'I eat what I see'!"

"You might just as well say," added the March Hare, "that 'I like what I get' is the same thing as 'I get what I like'!"

"You might just as well say," added the Dormouse, which seemed to be talking in its sleep, "that 'I breathe when I sleep' is the same thing as 'I sleep when I breathe'!"

"It *is* the same thing with you," said the Hatter, and here the conversation dropped, and the party sat silent for a minute, while Alice thought over all she could remember about ravens and writing-desks, which wasn't much.

ALICE'S ADVENTURES IN WONDERLAND

1 large white loaf / 2 tablespoons sweet sherry / 2 eggs / ½ pound sifted icing sugar / cooking oil / 1 heaped tablespoon powdered cinnamon

1 Cut about 12 rounds of bread, one inch thick and devoid of crusts, from the loaf, using a pastry cutter about $2\frac{1}{2}$ inches in diameter.

2 Sift the icing sugar and cinnamon together.

3 Beat sherry and eggs together.

4 Bring oil to a moderate heat, about 380 degrees.

5 Dip each bread round into the egg mixture, and then immerse in the oil.

6 Fry until golden brown.

7 Dust each "mock" doughnut with the sugar mixture and serve at once, the ideal addition to a tea table like the Mad Hatter's where nothing is as it seems.

Treacle-Well Tart

"Tell us a story!" said the March Hare.

"Yes, please do!" pleaded Alice.

"And be quick about it," added the Hatter, "or you'll be asleep again before it's done."

"Once upon a time there were three little sisters," the Dormouse began in a great hurry; "and their names were Elsie, Lacie, and Tillie; and they lived at the bottom of a well—"

"What did they live on?" said Alice, who always took a great interest in questions of eating and drinking.

"They lived on treacle," said the Dormouse, after thinking a minute or two.

"They couldn't have done that, you know," Alice gently remarked. "They'd have been ill."

"So they were," said the Dormouse; "*very* ill."

Alice tried a little to fancy to herself what such an extraordinary way of living would be like, but it puzzled her too much: so she went on: "But why did they live at the bottom of a well?"

"Take some more tea," the March Hare said to Alice, very earnestly.

"I've had nothing yet," Alice replied in an offended tone: "so I can't take more."

"You mean you can't take *less*," said the Hatter: "it's very easy to take *more* than nothing."

"Nobody asked *your* opinion," said Alice.

"Who's making personal remarks now?" the Hatter asked triumphantly.

Alice did not quite know what to say to this: so she helped herself to some tea and bread-and-butter, and then turned to the Dormouse, and repeated her question. "Why did they live at the bottom of a well?"

The Dormouse again took a minute or two to think about it, and then said, "It was a treacle-well."

"There's no such thing!" Alice was beginning very angrily, but the Hatter and the March Hare went "Sh! Sh!" and the Dormouse sulkily remarked, "If you can't be civil, you'd better finish the story for yourself."

"No, please go on!" Alice said very humbly. "I won't interrupt you again. I dare say there may be *one*."

"One, indeed!" said the Dormouse indignantly. However, he consented to go on. "And so these three little sisters—they were learning to draw, you know—"

"What did they draw?" said Alice, quite forgetting her promise.

"Treacle," said the Dormouse, without considering at all this time.

"I want a clean cup," interrupted the Hatter: "let's all move one place on."

ALICE'S ADVENTURES IN WONDERLAND

43

½ pound plain flour / 2 ounces butter / 2 ounces lard / pinch of salt /
2½ tablespoons water—no more

1 Sift flour and salt together into a basin.

2 Cut the butter (for flavour) and lard (for texture) into smaller pieces, and then rub gently into the flour with the tips of the fingers until the mixture resembles the finest of breadcrumbs.

3 Sprinkle the water over the mixture and mix to a smooth, stiff dough.

4 Dust working surface with flour and roll out gently to desired thickness.

5 You are now ready to proceed with the treacle-well tart for which, in addition to shortcrust pastry, you will also need:
3 tablespoons fresh breadcrumbs /
1 tablespoon fresh orange juice /

grated rind of orange / 4 tablespoons golden syrup

6 Line a greased seven inch sandwich tin with pastry, trimming the edges and pressing down into the contours of the tin.

7 Add the breadcrumbs.

8 Sprinkle orange rind over the crumbs and then pour in the juice and treacle.

9 You can now use the pastry trimmings from Stage 6 to decorate the top with a lattice pattern.

10 Bake for approximately 25 minutes in an oven pre-heated to 425 degrees Fahrenheit, Gas Mark 6.

11 Serve hot or cold, but be careful not to fall down the well.

Milk-Jugged Hare

He moved on as he spoke, and the Dormouse followed him: the March Hare moved into the Dormouse's place, and Alice rather unwillingly took the place of the March Hare. The Hatter was the only one who got any advantage from the change; and Alice was a good deal worse off than before, as the March Hare had just upset the milk-jug into his plate.

ALICE'S ADVENTURES IN WONDERLAND

1 hare, jointed and bled by a friendly butcher / the resultant blood / ½ pound streaky bacon, chopped into cubes / ½ pound chopped onions / flour seasoned with herbs / 3 ounces lard / beef stock / port / redcurrant jelly / peppercorns / 1 bay leaf / ½ tablespoon chopped parsley

1 Wipe the pieces of hare with a damp cloth.

2 Roll them in the seasoned flour.

3 Melt the lard in a heavy-bottomed pan or casserole and then add hare, bacon and onions.

4 Brown them, turning continually for thoroughness.

5 Pour off any superfluous fat before adding peppercorns and assorted herbs.

6 Cover with stock and bring to the boil slowly.

7 You can now, if you wish, transfer everything to a large stoneware milk jug, from which the dish obtained its traditional name. Cover with cooking foil and stand in a pan of hot water. Alternatively, stay as you were at the end of Stage 6.

8 Simmer gently for two hours. You can tell that the meat is cooked when it parts easily from the bone.

9 Take off the heat and stir in the blood, together with the port to taste.

10 Keep just under boiling point for about five minutes, for sauce to thicken.

11 Serve with redcurrant jelly—left over from the Mad Hatter's tea party?

Sweet-Tempered Barley-Sugar

"You can't think how glad I am to see you again, you dear old thing!" said the Duchess, as she tucked her arm affectionately into Alice's, and they walked off together.

Alice was very glad to find her in such a pleasant temper, and thought to herself that perhaps it was only the pepper that had made her so savage when they met in the kitchen.

"When *I'm* a Duchess," she said to herself (not in a very hopeful tone, though), "I won't have any pepper in my kitchen *at all*. Soup does very well without—Maybe it's always pepper that makes people hot-tempered," she went on, very much pleased at having found out a new kind of rule, "and vinegar that makes them sour—and camomile that makes them bitter—and—and barley-sugar and such things that make children sweet-tempered. I only wish people knew *that*: then they wouldn't be so stingy about it, you know—"

ALICE'S ADVENTURES IN WONDERLAND

2 pounds sugar / 1 pint water / a candy thermometer / 1 teaspoon lemon juice / 5 drops lemon essence / saffron powder

1 Put sugar and water together into a saucepan.

2 Dissolve sugar and continue boiling until a syrup is formed.

3 When syrup reaches 312 degrees Fahrenheit, add both lemon juice and essence.

4 Keep boiling until syrup acquires a decided golden colour.

5 Then add saffron powder, stir, and almost immediately pour onto an oiled metal tray.

6 When cool cut into strips, which you can easily twist into traditional walking-stick shapes.

7 Store in air-tight tins to eat when you feel a tantrum coming on.

Hot-Tempered Mustard

"I dare say you're wondering why I don't put my arm round your waist," the Duchess said, after a pause: "the reason is, that I'm doubtful about the temper of your flamingo. Shall I try the experiment?"

"He might bite," Alice cautiously replied, not feeling at all anxious to have the experiment tried.

"Very true," said the Duchess: "flamingoes and mustard both bite. And the moral of that is—'Birds of a feather flock together.' "

"Only mustard isn't a bird," Alice remarked.

"Right, as usual," said the Duchess: "what a clear way you have of putting things!"

"It's a mineral, I *think*," said Alice.

"Of course it is," said the Duchess, who seemed ready to agree to everything that Alice said: "there's a large mustard-mine near here. And the moral of that is—'The more there is of mine, the less there is of yours.' "

"Oh, I know!" exclaimed Alice, who had not attended to this last remark, "it's a vegetable. It doesn't look like one, but it is."

"I quite agree with you," said the Duchess; "and the moral of that is—'Be what you would seem to be'—or, if you'd like it put more simply—'Never imagine yourself not to be otherwise than what it might appear to others that what you were or might have been was not otherwise than what you had been would have appeared to them to be otherwise.' "

ALICE'S ADVENTURES IN WONDERLAND

3 tablespoons mustard powder | 1 tablespoon castor sugar | 1 beaten egg |
½ pint pure malt vinegar | 1 tablespoon olive oil | 1 pinch of salt

1 Mix mustard, salt and sugar together in a basin.

2 Stir in the beaten egg until smooth.

3 Add the vinegar, beating until smooth.

4 Transfer to a saucepan and stir over a gentle heat for five minutes.

5 Leave to cool before stirring in the olive oil.

6 Serve with your favourite savoury dishes to make their appeal "otherwise" than what it might appear to have been.

Uncrumbed Whiting

So they began solemnly dancing round and round Alice, every now and then treading on her toes when they passed too close, and waving their fore-paws to mark the time, while the Mock Turtle sang this, very slowly and sadly:—

"Will you walk a little faster?" said a whiting to a snail,
"There's a porpoise close behind us, and he's treading on my tail.
See how eagerly the lobsters and the turtles all advance!
They are waiting on the shingle—will you come and join the dance?
   Will you, won't you, will you, won't you, will you join the dance?
   Will you, won't you, will you, won't you, won't you join the dance?

"You can really have no notion how delightful it will be
When they take us up and throw us, with the lobsters, out to sea!"
But the snail replied "Too far, too far!" and gave a look askance—
Said he thanked the whiting kindly, but he would not join the dance.
   Would not, could not, would not, could not, would not join the dance.
   Would not, could not, would not, could not, could not join the dance.

"What matters it how far we go?" his scaly friend replied.
"There is another shore, you know, upon the other side.
The further off from England the nearer is to France—
Then turn not pale, beloved snail, but come and join the dance.
   Will you, won't you, will you, won't you, will you join the dance?
   Will you, won't you, will you, won't you, won't you join the dance?"

"Thank you, it's a very interesting dance to watch," said Alice, feeling very glad that it was over at last: "and I do so like that curious song about the whiting!"

50

"Oh, as to the whiting," said the Mock Turtle, "they—you've seen them, of course?"

"Yes," said Alice, "I've often seen them at dinn—" she checked herself hastily.

"I don't know where Dinn may be," said the Mock Turtle; "but, if you've seen them so often, of course you know what they're like?"

"I believe so," Alice replied thoughtfully. "They have their tails in their mouths—and they're all over crumbs."

"You're wrong about the crumbs," said the Mock Turtle: "crumbs would all wash off in the sea. But they *have* their tails in their mouths; and the reason is—" here the Mock Turtle yawned and shut his eyes. "Tell her about the reason and all that," he said to the Gryphon.

"The reason is," said the Gryphon, "that they *would* go with the lobsters to the dance. So they got thrown out to sea. So they had to fall a long way. So they got their tails fast in their mouths. So they couldn't get them out again. That's all."

"Thank you," said Alice, "it's very interesting. I never knew so much about a whiting before."

ALICE'S ADVENTURES IN WONDERLAND

---

4 small whiting / 2 ounces finely chopped shallots / 2 ounces butter / ½ lemon / 1 tablespoon chopped parsley / 4 tablespoons white wine

1 Remove heads and fins from the fish and slit them along the backbone for the heat to penetrate easily.

2 Sprinkle the shallots upon a buttered fireproof dish.

3 Add the fish, followed by the wine and butter.

4 Bake in a moderate oven, temperature 375 degrees Fahrenheit, Gas Mark 5, for about 15–20 minutes, basting the fish with the juice at regular intervals.

5 By the time you come to serve, the liquid will almost certainly have evaporated. Sprinkle with lemon juice and parsley.

6 Crumbs, or no crumbs, it *is* a very interesting fish to eat.

Baked Lobster

"Stand up and repeat *'Tis the voice of the sluggard,'*" said the Gryphon.

"How the creatures order one about, and make one repeat· lessons!" thought Alice. "I might just as well be at school at once." However, she got up, and began to repeat it, but her head was so full of the Lobster-Quadrille, that she hardly knew what she was saying; and the words came very queer indeed:—

> " 'Tis the voice of the Lobster: I heard him declare.
> 'You have baked me too brown, I must sugar my hair.'
> As a duck with its eyelids, so he with his nose
> Trims his belt and his buttons, and turns out his toes.
> When the sands are all dry, he is gay as a lark,
> And will talk in contemptuous tones of the Shark:
> But, when the tide rises and sharks are around,
> His voice has a timid and tremulous sound."

"That's different from what *I* used to say when I was a child," said the Gryphon.

"Well, *I* never heard it before," said the Mock Turtle; "but it sounds uncommon nonsense."

ALICE'S ADVENTURES IN WONDERLAND

1 cooked lobster, about 2 pounds in weight / 1½ ounces butter / 2 teaspoons finely chopped shallots / ½ ounce flour / ½ pint milk / ½ lemon / 2 tablespoons finely chopped parsley / 1 egg yolk / ½ teaspoon anchovy essence / 4 tablespoons brown breadcrumbs / salt / pepper / parsley for garnish

1 Cut lobster into halves lengthwise.

2 Scoop out meat from the shells and chop into small pieces.

3 Melt butter in a pan and add the shallots.

4 Fry for about two minutes without browning.

5 Stir in flour and, away from the heat, the milk.

6 Return to the heat and stir until the mixture boils.

7 Boil for 5 minutes.

8 Add the juice of the lemon, the chopped parsley, and the anchovy essence. Also salt and pepper to taste.

9 Add the egg yolk, and stir without boiling until mixture begins to bind.

10 Mix in the lobster meat.

11 Clean the larger pieces of shell left over from Stage 2.

12 Spoon the mixture from pan to shell.

13 Sprinkle with breadcrumbs and then put 3 or 4 small pieces of butter on top of each dish.

14 Bake for 15–20 minutes in a moderate oven at 375 degrees Fahrenheit, Gas Mark 4 . . .

15 . . . but not *too* brown.

Owl
and Panther Pie

"Go on with the next verse," the Gryphon repeated: "it begins '*I passed by his garden.*'" Alice did not dare to disobey, though she felt sure it would all come wrong, and she went on in a trembling voice:—

> "I passed by his garden, and marked, with one eye,
> How the Owl and the Panther were sharing a pie:
> The Panther took pie-crust, and gravy, and meat,
> While the Owl had the dish as its share of the treat.
> When the pie was all finished, the Owl, as a boon,
> Was kindly permitted to pocket the spoon:
> While the Panther received knife and fork with a growl,
> And concluded the banquet by—"

"What *is* the use of repeating all that stuff," the Mock Turtle interrupted, "if you don't explain it as you go on? It's by far the most confusing thing *I* ever heard!"

"Yes, I think you'd better leave off," said the Gryphon, and Alice was only too glad to do so.

ALICE'S ADVENTURES IN WONDERLAND

shortcrust pastry (for which see Page 44) / 1 knuckle of veal sawn into three pieces by that obliging butcher / 1 pound stewing veal / 1 pound unsmoked ham / 3 hard-boiled eggs / 2 bay leaves / 1 teaspoon lemon juice / 1 quartered onion / 1 tablespoon mixed herbs / pepper / salt / milk

1 Immerse veal bones in water, to which the lemon juice has been added, and stew until soft.

2 Chop ham and veal into small cubes and put pieces into an earthenware stew jar or casserole.

3 Add the herbs, quartered onion and pepper to taste.

4 Cover with the stock from the bones and cook until meat is tender.

5 Add salt to taste.

6 Cut the hard-boiled eggs into halves.

7 Arrange meat and egg-halves in a pie dish, discarding the bay leaves and onion.

8 Cover again with the liquor.

9 If filling is not sufficient to fill dish to brim, put a pie funnel or inverted egg cup in the middle.

10 Add the pie crust, about $\frac{1}{4}$ inch thick.

11 Trim edges of pastry leaving $\frac{1}{2}$ inch overhanging the edge of the dish.

12 Tuck this in and press down against edge of dish.

13 Crimp edges all round with a wet fork.

14 Make 2 slits in the top of the pie for steam to escape.

15 Brush the top with milk.

16 Bake in a hot oven at 475 degrees Fahrenheit, Gas Mark 8, for 20 to 30·minutes or until pie crust is cooked.

17 Serve pie hot or cold, sharing *equally*.

Mock Turtle Soup

Then the Queen left off, quite out of breath, and said to Alice, "Have you seen the Mock Turtle yet?"

"No," said Alice. "I don't even know what a Mock Turtle is."

"It's the thing Mock Turtle Soup is made from," said the Queen.

"I never saw one, or heard of one," said Alice.

★   ★   ★   ★   ★

"Shall we try another figure of the Lobster-Quadrille?" the Gryphon went on. "Or would you like the Mock Turtle to sing you another song?"

"Oh, a song, please, if the Mock Turtle would be so kind," Alice replied, so eagerly that the Gryphon said, in a rather offended tone, "Hm! No accounting for tastes! Sing her '*Turtle Soup*,' will you, old fellow?"

The Mock Turtle sighed deeply, and began, in a voice choked with sobs, to sing this:—

"Beautiful Soup, so rich and green,
Waiting in a hot tureen!
Who for such dainties would not stoop?
Soup of the evening, beautiful Soup!
Soup of the evening, beautiful Soup!

  Beau—ootiful Soo—oop!
  Beau—ootiful Soo—oop!
Soo—oop of the e—e—evening,
  Beautiful, beautiful Soup!

"Beautiful Soup! Who cares for fish,
Game, or any other dish?
Who would not give all else for two p
ennyworth only of Beautiful Soup?
Pennyworth only of beautiful Soup?

  Beau—ootiful Soo—oop!
  Beau—ootiful Soo—oop!
Soo—oop of the e—e—evening,
  Beautiful, beauti-FUL SOUP!"

ALICE'S ADVENTURES IN WONDERLAND

58

½ *calf's head (note the Mock Turtle's head, hind hoofs and tail in the illustrations) / 2 quarts stock / ¼ pound cooked ham / 2½ ounces flour / 6 peppercorns / 3 cloves / sherry / herbs / 2 tablespoons mushroom ketchup / lemon rind / salt / pepper*

1 Cook the calf's head in the stock with herbs according to taste, cloves, sliver of lemon rind, peppercorns and ham.

2 When meat is tender, remove the ham and chop into small pieces.

3 Remove the head and separate the meat from the bone.

4 Chop half of the meat into small pieces and add to the ham. The veal left over can be used in another dish.

5 Return bones to pan, simmering gently for an hour.

6 Strain the liquor.

7 Add flour and thicken.

8 Add two glasses of sherry and mushroom ketchup, if obtainable.

9 Also salt and pepper to taste.

10 Finally add the small pieces of meat.

11 For traditional effect arrange two sliced hard-boiled eggs on the bottom of the tureen before pouring in the soup.

12 This makes an already beautiful soup look even more beauti-FUL!

The Jam Tarts
of the
Queen of Hearts

The King and Queen of Hearts were seated on their throne when they arrived, with a great crowd assembled about them—all sorts of little birds and beasts, as well as the whole pack of cards: the Knave was standing before them, in chains, with a soldier on each side to guard him; and near the King was the White Rabbit, with a trumpet in one hand, and a scroll of parch-

ment in the other. In the very middle of the court was a table, with a large dish of tarts upon it: they looked so good, that it made Alice quite hungry to look at them—"I wish they'd get the trial done," she thought, "and hand round the refreshments!" But there seemed to be no chance of this; so she began looking at everything about her to pass away the time.

*   *   *   *   *

"Herald, read the accusation!" said the King.

On this the White Rabbit blew three blasts on the trumpet, and then unrolled the parchment-scroll, and read as follows:—

"The Queen of Hearts, she made some tarts,
   All on a summer day:
The Knave of Hearts, he stole those tarts
   And took them quite away!"

ALICE'S ADVENTURES IN WONDERLAND

shortcrust pastry (for which see Page 44) / jam

1 Roll out pastry until about $\frac{1}{4}$ inch thick.

2 With a pastry cutter cut into rounds a little larger than the greased tins in which they'll be cooked.

3 Press each round into its tin.

4 Put a little jam on each round.

5 Sprinkle a thin layer of water onto the jam, to prevent jam drying out during cooking.

6 Bake for 10–15 minutes until lightly browned, in a moderately hot oven at 425 degrees Fahrenheit, Gas Mark 6.

7 To check if thoroughly cooked, lift a tart from the tin and look at its base.

8 Cool on a cake rack and keep under a close guard.

Looking-Glass
Milk

"How would you like to live in Looking-glass House, Kitty? I wonder if they'd give you milk in there? Perhaps Looking-glass milk isn't good to drink—but oh, Kitty! now we come to the passage. You can just see a little *peep* of the passage in Looking-glass House, if you leave the door of our drawing-room wide open: and it's very like our passage as far as you can see, only you know it may be quite different on beyond. Oh, Kitty, how nice it would be if we could only get through into Looking-glass House! I'm sure it's got, oh! such beautiful things in it! Let's pretend there's a way of getting through into it, somehow, Kitty. Let's pretend the glass has got all soft like gauze, so that we can get through. Why, it's turning into a sort of mist now, I declare! It'll be easy enough to get through—" She was up on the chimney-piece while she said this, though she hardly knew how she had got there. And certainly the glass *was* beginning to melt away, just like a bright silvery mist.

In another moment Alice was through the glass, and had jumped lightly down into the Looking-glass room.

THROUGH THE LOOKING-GLASS

1 pint cold milk / 1 pint ice-cream / flavouring of your choice: mashed banana; blackcurrant syrup; instant coffee with sugar to taste; apricot purée; chocolate powder / lots of time for experiment!

1 Slice ice-cream into small chunks.

2 Place in a large screw-topped jar.

3 Add chosen flavour and milk.

4 Screw on lid and shake vigorously until frothy.

5 Pour into tumblers to serve.

6 This looking-glass milk is decidedly good for you, unlike that queried by Alice which, as scientists have proved, would in real life have shaken up Alice herself, milk and girl exploding at the moment of contact on account of their asymmetrically opposed organic natures!

Very Dry Biscuits

"A slow sort of country!" said the Queen. "Now, *here*, you see, it takes all the running *you* can do, to keep in the same place. If you want to get somewhere else, you must run at least twice at fast as that."

"I'd rather not try, please!" said Alice. "I'm quite content to stay here— only I *am* so hot and thirsty!"

"I know what *you'd* like!" the Queen said good-naturedly, taking a little box out of her pocket. "Have a biscuit?"

Alice thought it would not be civil to say "No," though it wasn't at all what she wanted. So she took it, and ate it as well as she could: and it was *very* dry: and she thought she had never been so nearly choked in all her life.

"While you're refreshing yourself," said the Queen, "I'll just take the measurements." And she took a ribbon out of her pocket, marked in inches, and began measuring the ground, and sticking little pegs in here and there.

"At the end of two yards," she said, putting in a peg to mark the distance, "I shall give you your directions—have another biscuit?"

"No, thank you," said Alice: "one's *quite* enough!"

"Thirst quenched, I hope?" said the Queen.

THROUGH THE LOOKING-GLASS

---

4 ounces castor sugar | 4 ounces butter | 1 beaten egg | ½ pound flour | 1 lemon | a pinch of salt | a grating of nutmeg

1 With butter and sugar both at room temperature, beat them together in a warm basin until the mixture is soft and light and resembles whipped cream.

2 Beat in the already beaten egg.

3 Sift in the flour.

4 Add nutmeg, salt and the grated rind of the lemon.

5 Mix to a stiff paste.

6 Roll out thinly on a lightly floured working surface.

7 Cut into whatever shapes take your fancy—say, hearts and diamonds, clubs and spades.

8 Prick them all over with a pin.

9 Place on an oiled tray and bake in a slow moderate oven at 325 degrees Fahrenheit, Gas Mark 3, until lightly brown.

10 Take care they do not emerge *too* dry.

69

Snapdragon

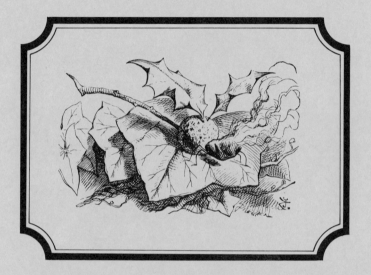

"Look on the branch above your head," said the Gnat, "and there you'll find a Snap-dragon fly. Its body is made of plum-pudding, its wings of holly-leaves, and its head is a raisin burning in brandy."

"And what does it live on?" Alice asked, as before.

"Frumenty and mince-pie," the Gnat replied; "and it makes its nest in a Christmas-box."

"And then there's the Butterfly," Alice went on, after she had taken a good look at the insect with its head on fire, and had thought to herself, "I wonder if that's the reason insects are so fond of flying into candles—because they want to turn into Snap-dragon-flies!"

THROUGH THE LOOKING-GLASS

a shallow metal bowl / brandy / seeded raisins

1 For this traditional Victorian Christmas game, rather than dish, fill the bowl with brandy, toss in the raisins, and then set light to the spirit.

2 The object of the game (also known as Flapdragon) is to snatch the raisins from the flickering blue flames and pop them, still alight, into your mouth.

3 For full atmospheric effect the room should be otherwise in darkness, while to ensure the longest lasting flames none of the flavour is impaired if the brandy is beforehand diluted with vodka, two parts of the former to one of the latter.

4 The flavour of the raisins is enhanced, in fact, if they are steeped in a jar of the spirit for a day or two before playing the game.

Frumenty and Mince Pie

"And what does it live on?" Alice asked, as before.

"Frumenty and mince-pie," the Gnat replied; "and it makes its nest in a Christmas-box."

THROUGH THE LOOKING–GLASS

Frumenty

*4 ounces wheat germ: e.g. Froment, available at all health food stores /
1 pint and 2 tablespoons milk / 2 ounces raisins / 2 teaspoons flour /
a pinch of cinnamon / $\frac{1}{4}$ teaspoon grated nutmeg / 1–2 tablespoons honey /
cream*

1 To make a modern version of this mediæval dish, long served alongside roast venison; but equally enjoyable on its own, heat the pint of milk gently in a saucepan.

2 Stir in the wheat germ gradually.

3 Mix the flour into a paste with the remaining milk and add to the saucepan.

4 Stirring, bring to the boil.

5 Still stirring, reduce heat and cook for 5 minutes.

6 Add raisins, honey, nutmeg and cinnamon.

7 Serve in individual dishes with cream according to taste.

72

Mince-Pie

1½ pounds sharp apples / 1 orange / 1 lemon / 1 tangerine / 1 pound currants / ½ pound raisins / 1 pound sultanas / 4 ounces mixed peel / 4 ounces almonds / 1 pound shredded suet / ¾ pound soft brown sugar / 1 teaspoon ground ginger / 1 teaspoon ground nutmeg / 1 teaspoon cinnamon / 5 tablespoons brandy / 5 tablespoons rum

1 Carefully peel and core the apples, then chop finely.

2 Skin almonds by steeping them in boiling water, and again chop into small pieces.

3 Stir apples, almonds, assorted dry fruit, peel and suet together in a large mixing bowl.

4 Add both the grated rind and the juice of the 3 citrus fruits, together with the sugar and spices.

5 Mix thoroughly.

6 Add spirits last, stirring well.

7 Leave in a cool place for two days and then store in sealed preserving jars.

8 For best results keep for at least a month before using in the mince-pie,

for which you'll also need:
shortcrust pastry (for which see page 44 / castor sugar / a jug of water

9 Line a sandwich tin with pastry, as for "Treacle-Well Tart".

10 Fill the pastry with mincemeat.

11 Cover with more pastry, trimming and crimping the edges.

12 Make 2 or 3 slits in the top to let out the steam and bake in a moderately hot oven at 425 degrees Fahrenheit, Gas Mark 6, for between 40 and 50 minutes until pastry is golden brown.

13 Dredge with sugar to serve hot or cold.

14 The water is for warding off preying Snap-dragon-flies.

Bread-and-Butter-Fly
Pudding

"Crawling at your feet," said the Gnat (Alice drew her feet back in some alarm), "you may observe a Bread-and-butter-fly. Its wings are thin slices of bread-and-butter, its body is a crust, and its head is a lump of sugar."

"And what does *it* live on?"

"Weak tea with cream in it."

A new difficulty came into Alice's head. "Supposing it couldn't find any?" she suggested.

"Then it would die, of course."

"But that must happen very often," Alice remarked thoughtfully.

"It always happens," said the Gnat.

THROUGH THE LOOKING-GLASS

74

6 slices thin bread and butter / 1 pint milk / 2 ounces currants / 2 ounces sultanas / 2 ounces sugar / 2 eggs / ½ teaspoon vanilla essence / nutmeg / salt / butter

1 Generously daub the inside of a pie-dish with butter.

2 Arrange the slices of bread and butter, minus their crusts, in layers in the dish, sprinkling the sugar, currants and sultanas in between.

3 Flavour milk with vanilla and a pinch of salt.

4 Beat the eggs and whisk in milk.

5 Pour the liquid over the bread and leave to stand for ten minutes.

6 Sprinkle with grated nutmeg.

7 Cook in a moderately slow oven at 325 degrees Fahrenheit, Gas Mark 3, for about an hour, until the top is crispy and the egg mixture lightly set.

8 Serve with cream without weak tea.

An Oyster Banquet

The sun was shining on the sea,
   Shining with all his might:
He did his very best to make
   The billows smooth and bright—
And this was odd, because it was
   The middle of the night.

The moon was shining sulkily,
   Because she thought the sun
Had got no business to be there
   After the day was done—
'It's very rude of him,' she said,
   'To come and spoil the fun!'

The sea was wet as wet could be,
   The sands were dry as dry.
You could not see a cloud, because
   No cloud was in the sky:
No birds were flying overhead—
   There were no birds to fly.

The Walrus and the Carpenter
  Were walking close at hand:
They wept like anything to see
  Such quantities of sand:
'If this were only cleared away,'
  They said, 'it would be grand!'

'If seven maids with seven mops
  Swept it for half a year,
Do you suppose,' the Walrus said,
  'That they could get it clear?'
'I doubt it,' said the Carpenter,
  And shed a bitter tear.

'O Oysters, come and walk with us!'
  The Walrus did beseech.
'A pleasant walk, a pleasant talk,
  Along the briny beach:
We cannot do with more than four,
  To give a hand to each.'

The eldest Oyster looked at him,
  But never a word he said:
The eldest Oyster winked his eye,
  And shook his heavy head—
Meaning to say he did not choose
  To leave the oyster-bed.

But four young Oysters hurried up,
  All eager for the treat:
Their coats were brushed, their faces washed,
  Their shoes were clean and neat—
And this was odd, because, you know,
  They hadn't any feet.

Four other Oysters followed them,
  And yet another four;
And thick and fast they came at last,
  And more, and more, and more—
All hopping through the frothy waves,
  And scrambling to the shore.

The Walrus and the Carpenter
  Walked on a mile or so,
And then they rested on a rock
  Conveniently low:
And all the little Oysters stood
  And waited in a row.

'The time has come,' the Walrus said,
    'To talk of many things:
Of shoes—and ships—and sealing-wax—
    Of cabbages—and kings—
And why the sea is boiling hot—
    And whether pigs have wings.'

'But wait a bit,' the Oysters cried,
    'Before we have our chat;
For some of us are out of breath,
    And all of us are fat!'
'No hurry!' said the Carpenter.
    They thanked him much for that.

'A loaf of bread,' the Walrus said,
  'Is what we chiefly need:
Pepper and vinegar besides
  Are very good indeed—
Now, if you're ready, Oysters dear,
  We can begin to feed.'

'But not on us!' the Oysters cried,
  Turning a little blue.
'After such kindness, that would be
  A dismal thing to do!'
'The night is fine,' the Walrus said.
  'Do you admire the view?

'It was so kind of you to come!
  And you are very nice!'
The Carpenter said nothing but
  'Cut us another slice.
I wish you were not quite so deaf—
  I've had to ask you twice!'

'It seems a shame,' the Walrus said,
  'To play them such a trick.
After we've brought them out so far,
  And made them trot so quick!'
The Carpenter said nothing but
  'The butter's spread too thick!'

'I weep for you,' the Walrus said:
  'I deeply sympathize.'
With sobs and tears he sorted out
  Those of the largest size,
Holding his pocket-handkerchief
  Before his streaming eyes.

'O Oysters,' said the Carpenter,
  'You've had a pleasant run!
Shall we be trotting home again?'
  But answer came there none—
And this was scarcely odd, because
  They'd eaten every one.

THROUGH THE LOOKING-GLASS

oysters / thin brown bread and butter / cayenne pepper / lemon juice

1 Scrub the oysters thoroughly under a cold tap.

2 Wrap your left hand (or your right if you are left-handed) in a cloth and use it to hold the oyster, with its deeper shell downwards, firmly against your working surface, its hinge end pointing towards your right.

3 Insert the point of a short, sharp knife between the two shells at the hinge end and gently feel along the flat shell until the valve is detached.

4 Lever the oyster open.

5 Serve the flesh and its juices in the deeper shell on a bed of crushed ice and seaweed.

6 The accompaniments listed above are not only traditional, but *de rigueur*, like the tradition which says they should be eaten raw. Other than that there is little more to say, and no reason why the White Queen should not be given the last word:

The White Queen laughed with delight, and stroked Alice's cheek. Then she began:

> " 'First, the fish must be caught.'
> That is easy: a baby, I think, could have caught it.
> 'Next, the fish must be bought.'
> That is easy: a penny, I think, would have bought it.
>
> 'Now cook me the fish!'
> That is easy, and will not take more than a minute.
> 'Let it lie in a dish!'
> That is easy, because it already is in it.

'Bring it here! Let me sup!'
It is easy to set such a dish on the table.
   'Take the dish-cover up!'
Ah, *that* is so hard that I fear I'm unable!

   For it holds it like glue—
Holds the lid to the dish, while it lies in the middle:
   Which is easiest to do,
Un-dish-cover the fish, or dishcover the riddle?"

"Take a minute to think about it, and then guess," said the Red Queen.

7 One answer was volunteered
anonymously in the October 30th,
1878 edition of *Fun* magazine:

   Get an oyster-knife strong,
Insert it 'twixt cover and dish in the middle;
   Then you shall before long
Un-dish-cover the OYSTERS—dish-cover the riddle!

Jam Tomorrow
and Jam Yesterday

Alice carefully released the brush, and did her best to get the hair into order. "Come, you look rather better now!" she said, after altering most of the pins. "But really you should have a lady's-maid!"

"I'm sure I'll take *you* with pleasure!" the Queen said. "Twopence a week, and jam every other day."

Alice couldn't help laughing, as she said "I don't want you to hire *me*—and I don't care for jam."

"It's very good jam," said the Queen.

"Well, I don't want any *to-day*, at any rate."

84

"You couldn't have it if you *did* want it," the Queen said. "The rule is, jam to-morrow and jam yesterday—but never jam *to-day*."

"It *must* come sometimes to 'jam today,'" Alice objected.

"No, it can't," said the Queen. "It's jam every *other* day: to-day isn't any *other* day, you know."

"I don't understand you," said Alice. "It's dreadfully confusing!"

That's the effect of living backwards," the Queen said kindly: "it always makes one a little giddy at first—"

"Living backwards!" Alice repeated in great astonishment. "I never heard of such a thing!"

THROUGH THE LOOKING-GLASS

---

plums / sugar (allow one pound of sugar for each pound of fruit) / water / a pinch of salt

1 Halve plums, removing stalks and stones.

2 Put fruit into a preserving pan with sugar, salt and no more than $\frac{1}{4}$ pint of water for each pound of fruit—in fact less, and sometimes none at all, if the plums are running a considerable amount of juice.

3 Bring gently to the boil.

4 Simmer slowly for 30 minutes and then boil rapidly, stirring all the time, until setting point is reached . . . see Lewis Carroll's Oxford Marmalade, Page 19.

5 Remove any scum that may have risen to the top.

6 Allow to cool a little and then pot in dry, warm jars, as if it were marmalade—all dreadfully confusing!

Very Pretty Eggs

"And how exactly like an egg he is!" she said aloud, standing with her hands ready to catch him, for she was every moment expecting him to fall.

"It's *very* provoking," Humpty Dumpty said after a long silence, looking away from Alice as he spoke, "to be called an egg,—*very*!"

"I said you *looked* like an egg, Sir," Alice gently explained. "And some eggs are very pretty, you know," she added, hoping to turn her remark into a sort of compliment.

"Some people," said Humpty Dumpty, looking away from her as usual, "have no more sense than a baby!"

THROUGH THE LOOKING GLASS

86

6 hard-boiled eggs / 1 pint boiling water / 1½ tablespoons orange pekoe tea / ¼ teaspoon aniseed / 2 tablespoons soy sauce / ¾ tablespoon salt

1 Pour boiling water over tea, let stand for 5 minutes, then strain.

2 Stir in aniseed, soy sauce and salt.

3 Cover the shells of the eggs in small cracks by rolling them gently on the table.

4 Simmer (but do *not* boil) the eggs in this condition for an hour in the mixture.

5 Remove the shells (or leave for guests to do themselves at the table) and the surface of the eggs will magically resemble antique cracked porcelain—not that this would have been of much consolation to Humpty Dumpty when *he* cracked all over.

Ham Sandwich Butter
with an 'H'

"This young lady loves you with an H," the King said, introducing Alice in the hope of turning off the Messenger's attention from himself—but it was of no use—the Anglo-Saxon attitudes only got more extraordinary every moment, while the great eyes rolled wildly from side to side.

"You alarm me!" said the King. "I feel faint—Give me a ham sandwich!"

On which the Messenger, to Alice's great amusement, opened a bag that hung round his neck, and handed a sandwich to the King, who devoured it greedily.

"Another sandwich!" said the King.

"There's nothing but hay left now," the Messenger said, peeping into the bag.

"Hay, then," the King murmured in a faint whisper.

Alice was glad to see that it revived him a good deal. "There's nothing like eating hay when you're faint," he remarked to her, as he munched away.

"I should think throwing cold water over you would be better," Alice suggested: "—or some sal-volatile."

"I didn't say there was nothing *better*," the King replied. "I said there was nothing *like* it." Which Alice did not venture to deny.

THROUGH THE LOOKING-GLASS

---

4 ounces finely chopped ham / 2 ounces soft butter / 1 tablespoon double cream / cayenne pepper

1 With a pestle and mortar pound ham to a smooth consistency, adding some of the butter to make for ease of working.

2 Pass mixture through a fine sieve.

3 Blend in the cream and the rest of the butter.

4 Add enough cayenne to taste . . .

5 . . . and some more still to combat fainting.

Portmanteau Bread

"I'll whisper it," said the Messenger, putting his hands to his mouth in the shape of a trumpet and stooping so as to get close to the King's ear. Alice was sorry for this, as she wanted to hear the news too. However, instead of whispering, he simply shouted, at the top of his voice, "They're at it again!"

"Do you call *that* a whisper?" cried the poor King, jumping up and shaking himself. "If you do such a thing again, I'll have you buttered! It went through and through my head like an earthquake!"

"It would have to be a very tiny earthquake!" thought Alice. "Who are at it again?" she ventured to ask.

"Why, the Lion and the Unicorn, of course," said the King.

"Fighting for the crown?"

90

"Yes, to be sure," said the King: "and the best of the joke is, that it's *my* crown all the while! Let's run and see them." And they trotted off, Alice repeating to herself, as she ran, the words of the old song:

> "The Lion and the Unicorn were fighting for the crown:
> The Lion beat the Unicorn all round the town.
> Some gave them white bread, some gave them brown:
> Some gave them plum-cake and drummed them out of town."

"Does—the one—that wins—get the crown?" she asked, as well as she could, for the run was putting her quite out of breath.

"Dear me, no!" said the King. "What an idea!"

★   ★   ★   ★   ★

They placed themselves close to where Hatta, the other Messenger, was standing watching the fight, with a cup of tea in one hand and a piece of bread-and-butter in the other.

"He's only just out of prison, and he hadn't finished his tea when he was sent in," Haigha whispered to Alice: "and they only give them oyster-shells in there—so you see he's very hungry and thirsty. How are you, dear child?" he went on, putting his arm affectionately round Hatta's neck.

Hatta looked round and nodded, and went on with his bread-and-butter.

"Were you happy in prison, dear child?" said Haigha.

Hatta looked round once more, and this time a tear or two trickled down his cheek; but not a word would he say.

"Speak, can't you!" Haigha cried impatiently. But Hatta only munched away, and drank some more tea.

"Speak, won't you!" cried the King. "How are they getting on with the fight?"

Hatta made a desperate effort, and swallowed a large piece of bread-and-butter. "They're getting on very well," he said in a choking voice: "each of them has been down about eighty-seven times."

"Then I suppose they'll soon bring the white bread and the brown?" Alice ventured to remark.

"It's waiting for 'em now," said Hatta; "this is a bit of it as I'm eating."

There was a pause in the fight just then, and the Lion and the Unicorn sat down, panting, while the King called out "Ten minutes allowed for refreshments!" Haigha and Hatta set to work at once, carrying round trays of white and brown bread. Alice took a piece to taste, but it was *very* dry.

"I don't think they'll fight any more to-day," the King said to Hatta: "go and order the drums to begin." And Hatta went bounding away like a grasshopper.

THROUGH THE LOOKING-GLASS

1½ pounds white flour / 1 pound wholemeal flour / 2 ounces butter or margarine / ½ ounce dried yeast / ½ ounce salt / 1½ pints warm water

1 Mix the yeast with a little of the water.

2 Sift the flour and salt into a large mixing bowl.

3 Make a well in the centre and pour in the yeast mixture.

4 Melt the butter and add to the flour.

5 Pour in the water, a little at a time, blending all the ingredients thoroughly with the finger-tips.

6 Continue to knead the resultant dough with your hands, folding, stretching and pummelling it for about 15 to 20 minutes until it possesses an elastic putty-like consistency.

7 Cover the bowl with a damp cloth and place in a warm place for the dough to rise. This should take about two hours, by the end of which the dough will have doubled in size. Alternatively, leave the dough to rise overnight.

8 When it has risen, knead again lightly and divide into quarters. Press the loaves into four well-oiled bread tins, or arrange them, shaped appropriately, on an oiled metal baking tray.

9 Leave in a moderately warm atmosphere again for 45 to 60 minutes. Too much heat will kill the yeast. This stage is called "proving" and is over when the dough, again increased in size, yields as slightly puffy to the touch.

92

10 Bake in an oven pre-heated to 450 degrees Fahrenheit, Gas Mark 8, for about 45 minutes. The test of whether a loaf is cooked is to tap it on the bottom (after it has been removed from the tin!). If it sounds hollow, it's ready.

11 If so, place on a wire rack to cool.

12 The title? Just as Carroll invented so many "portmanteau" words, ingenious combinations of two meanings packed into one word, like "slithy" for "lithe and slimy" and frumious for "fuming and furious", so, in honour of the lion and the unicorn, one now offers two breads, "white and brown", packed into one loaf.

Looking-Glass Cake

"Come, fetch out the plum-cake, old man!" the Unicorn went on, turning from her to the King. "None of your brown bread for me!"

★   ★   ★   ★   ★

Alice had seated herself on the bank of a little brook, with the great dish on her knees, and was sawing away diligently with the knife. "It's very provoking!" she said, in reply to the Lion (she was getting quite used to being called 'the Monster'). "I've cut several slices already, but they always join on again!"

"You don't know how to manage Looking-glass cakes," the Unicorn remarked. "Hand it round first, and cut it afterwards."

This sounded nonsense, but Alice very obediently got up, and carried the dish round, and the cake divided itself into three pieces as she did so. "*Now* cut it up," said the Lion, as she returned to her place with the empty dish.

"I say, this isn't fair!" cried the Unicorn, as Alice sat with the knife in her hand, very much puzzled how to begin. "The Monster has given the Lion twice as much as me!"

"She's kept none for herself, anyhow," said the Lion. "Do you like plum-cake, Monster?"

But before Alice could answer him, the drums began.

THROUGH THE LOOKING-GLASS

94

1 pound flour / ½ pound butter / 4 ounces currants / 4 ounces mixed peel / 4 ounces raisins / ½ pound castor sugar / 2 teaspoons baking powder / 3 eggs / 1 teaspoon mixed spice / milk

1 Cream butter and sugar until fluffy, as in Stage 1 of *"Very* Dry Biscuits" on Page 68.

2 Beat eggs and whisk gradually into the creamed mixture.

3 Sift flour and baking powder and fold into the mixture by degrees.

4 Finally mix in fruit and spice.

5 The mixture should now be of such a consistency that it will drop easily from the spoon. Add milk only if necessary.

6 Turn into a cake tin approximately 7½ inches in diameter lined with greaseproof paper.

7 Bake for 2–3 hours in a slow oven at 300 degrees Fahrenheit, Gas Mark 2.

8 Test with a skewer to see if cooked. Insert it in the centre. If it comes out clean, the cake is ready to be placed on a wire rack to cool.

9 Cut it *first* and *hand round* afterwards.

Blotting-Paper Pudding

"How *can* you go on talking so quietly, head downwards?" Alice asked, as she dragged him out by the feet, and laid him in a heap on the bank.

The Knight looked surprised at the question. "What does it matter where my body happens to be?" he said. "My mind goes on working all the same. In fact, the more head downwards I am, the more I keep inventing new things.

"Now the cleverest thing of the sort that I ever did," he went on after a pause, "was inventing a new pudding during the meat-course."

"In time to have it cooked for the next course?" said Alice. "Well, that *was* quick work, certainly!"

"Well, not the *next* course," the Knight said in a slow thoughtful tone: "no, certainly not the next *course*."

"Then it would have to be the next day. I suppose you wouldn't have two pudding courses in one dinner?"

"Well, not the *next* day," the Knight repeated as before: "not the next *day*. In fact," he went on, holding his head down, and his voice getting lower and lower, "I don't believe that pudding ever *was* cooked! In fact, I don't believe that pudding ever *will* be cooked! And yet it was a very clever pudding to invent."

"What did you mean it to be made of?" Alice asked, hoping to cheer him up, for the poor Knight seemed quite low-spirited about it.

"It began with blotting-paper," the Knight answered with a groan.

"That wouldn't be very nice, I'm afraid—"

"Not very nice *alone*," he interrupted, quite eagerly: "but you've no idea what a difference it makes, mixing it with other things—such as gunpowder and sealing wax. And here I must leave you." They had just come to the end of the wood.

Alice could only look puzzled: she was thinking of the pudding.

THROUGH THE LOOKING-GLASS

1½ ounces rice / ½ ounce sugar / 1 pint milk / a sliver of lemon rind / a pinch of salt / a knob of butter / grated nutmeg

1 Sprinkle rice, which should be thoroughly cleaned, into a baking dish.

2 Add sugar, salt and lemon.

3 Pour on milk and toss in butter.

4 Sprinkle nutmeg over the top.

5 Bake very, very slowly for 2 to 3 hours at 300 degrees Fahrenheit, Gas Mark 2.

6 If you like yours creamy, stir in the skin several times during the early stages of cooking.

7 Then leave well alone to produce a crispy black skin on top.

8 One is assuming that the White Knight meant rice-blotting-paper!

Fratters

But I was thinking of a way
　To feed oneself on batter,
And so go on from day to day
　Getting a little fatter.
I shook him well from side to side,
　Until his face was blue:
'Come, tell me how you live,' I cried,
　'And what it is you do!'

THROUGH THE LOOKING-GLASS

---

4 ounces flour / 1 tablespoon olive or vegetable oil / $\frac{1}{4}$ pint warm water / 2 egg whites / 1 teaspoon salt / fruit of your choice, ideally apple rings; bananas halved lengthwise; pineapple slices; stoned cherries kept on the stem / castor sugar / cooking oil

1 Sift flour and salt into a basin.

2 Mix into a smooth paste with the oil and water.

3 Whisk egg whites and fold lightly into batter.

4 Take each piece of fruit on the point of a skewer (except the cherries) and dip into batter, coating thoroughly and draining off the surplus.

5 Lift out and drop into a pan of hot deep oil (approximately 340 degrees Fahrenheit). You can tell if the oil is hot enough by dropping in a teaspoon of batter. If it sizzles, rises to the surface and begins to turn brown, the temperature is correct.

6 Fry until golden brown all over, turning fritter at least once in the process.

7 Drain on absorbent kitchen paper and dredge with castor sugar.

8 Serve hot with lemon juice.

9 The title is an attempt to out-portmanteau Carroll: fruit and batter and fritter and fatter, four meanings all in one word.

100

Flower
Salad

"Of course you know your A B C?" said the Red Queen.

"To be sure I do," said Alice.

"So do I," the White Queen whispered: "we'll often say it over together, dear. And I'll tell you a secret—I can read words of one letter! Isn't *that* grand? However, don't be discouraged. You'll come to it in time."

Here the Red Queen began again. "Can you answer useful questions?" she said. "How is bread made?"

"I know *that*!" Alice cried eagerly. "You take some flour—"

"Where do you pick the flower?" the White Queen asked. "In a garden or in the hedges?"

"Well, it isn't *picked* at all," Alice explained: "it's *ground*—"

"How many acres of ground?" said the White Queen. "You musn't leave out so many things."

THROUGH THE LOOKING-GLASS

acacia flowers / marrow flowers / rosemary flowers / borage flowers / cowslip flowers / elderflowers / marigold petals / nasturtium petals and trumpets / green salad / olive oil / vinegar

1 All the flowers listed were once commonly accepted for culinary purposes. So:

2 Scald the petals with hot water.

3 Leave to cool.

4 Arrange a bed of green salad including lettuce, parsley, thyme, chives, sorrel leaves, sliced raw cabbage or spinach, according to availability.

5 Add the flowers to the centre.

6 Serve with oil and vinegar dressing, proof that some flowers, at least, *do* have the edible qualities of the other *flour*.

A Toast to Alice

At this moment the door was flung open, and a shrill voice was heard singing:—

"To the Looking-Glass world it was Alice that said
'I've a sceptre in hand, I've a crown on my head.
Let the Looking-Glass creatures, whatever they be
Come and dine with the Red Queen, the White Queen and me!' "

And hundreds of voices joined in the chorus:—

"Then fill up the glasses as quick as you can,
And sprinkle the table with buttons and bran:
Put cats in the coffee, and mice in the tea—
And welcome Queen Alice with thirty-times-three!"

Then followed a confused noise of cheering, and Alice thought to herself "Thirty times three makes ninety. I wonder if any one's counting?" In a minute there was silence again, and the same shrill voice sang another verse:—

" 'O Looking-Glass creatures,' quoth Alice, 'draw near!
'Tis an honour to see me, a favour to hear:
'Tis a privilege high to have dinner and tea
Along with the Red Queen, the White Queen, and me!' "

Then came the chorus again:—

"Then fill up the glasses with treacle and ink,
Or anything else that is pleasant to drink:
Mix sand with the cider, and wool with the wine—
And welcome Queen Alice with ninety-times-nine!"

THROUGH THE LOOKING GLASS

---

1 flagon cider / 8 lumps sugar / 2 oranges / 8 cloves / 1 teaspoon grated nutmeg / 1 cinnamon stick / 8 teaspoons water / 1 lemon / 1 sherry glass of rum / 1 sherry glass of brandy

1 Rub the sugar against the rind of one of the oranges to remove zest.

2 Cut this orange in half, and squeeze out juice into a saucepan.

3 Cut the other orange into 8 segments.

4 Stick a clove in each and sprinkle with nutmeg.

5 Add to the pan with the water and cinnamon.

6 Cut lemon rind into strips and add this also.

7 Heat over a gentle flame until sugar dissolves.

8 Simmer for 5 minutes.

9 Take away from heat to cool.

10 Remove cinnamon stick.

11 Add cider and reheat.

12 Add rum and brandy.

13 Serve hot in a heated punch bowl.

14 "And welcome Queen Alice with ninety-times-nine!"

Roast Leg of Mutton

There were three chairs at the head of the table: the Red and White Queens had already taken two of them, but the middle one was empty. Alice sat down in it, rather uncomfortable at the silence, and longing for some one to speak.

At last the Red Queen began. "You've missed the soup and fish," she said. "Put on the joint!" And the waiters set a leg of mutton before Alice, who looked at it rather anxiously, as she had never had to carve a joint before.

"You look a little shy: let me introduce you to that leg of mutton," said the Red Queen. "Alice—Mutton: Mutton—Alice." The leg of mutton got

106

up in a dish and made a little bow to Alice; and Alice returned the bow, not knowing whether to be frightened or amused.

"May I give you a slice?" she said, taking up the knife and fork, and looking from one Queen to the other.

"Certainly not," the Red Queen said, very decidedly: "it isn't etiquette to cut any one you've been introduced to. Remove the joint!" And the waiters carried it off, and brought a large plum-pudding in its place.

THROUGH THE LOOKING-GLASS

---

leg of mutton / flour / salt / pepper / herbs according to taste

1 Place meat in a deep baking-tin.

2 If lean, add some extra fat or dripping.

3 Sprinkle generously with salt, pepper and herbs.

4 Dredge with flour.

5 Put tin in a very hot oven, pre-heated to 500 degrees Fahrenheit, Gas Mark 10.

6 15 minutes at this heat will seal in the juices. Then lower temperature to 350 degrees, Gas Mark 4.

7 Continue to roast, basting meat with hot fat every 10 minutes.

8 The approximate time for roasting mutton is 20 to 25 minutes to the pound, and 20 to 25 minutes on top of that.

9 Half-way through your estimated timing, turn meat and dredge the lower side with flour.

10 When cooked, lift the meat out onto a serving dish.

11 Pour surplus fat from baking-tin into a basin until you are left with a brown sediment, the juice of the meat.

12 Place tin over a gentle flame and stir in $\frac{1}{2}$ saltspoon of salt and $\frac{1}{2}$ pint of boiling water or stock, dislodging any of the meat extract that adheres to the side of the tin. Voila—gravy!

13 Now turn back to the meat and carve politely.

Conjuring-Trick Pudding

"I won't be introduced to the pudding, please," Alice said rather hastily, "or we shall get no dinner at all. May I give you some?"

But the Red Queen looked sulky, and growled "Pudding—Alice: Alice—Pudding. Remove the pudding!" and the waiters took it away so quickly that Alice couldn't return its bow.

However, she didn't see why the Red Queen should be the only one to give orders; so, as an experiment, she called out "Waiter! Bring back the pudding!" and there it was again in a moment, like a conjuring-trick. It was so large that she couldn't help feeling a *little* shy with it, as she had been with the mutton: however, she conquered her shyness by a great effort, and cut a slice and handed it to the Red Queen.

"What impertinence!" said the Pudding. "I wonder how you'd like it, if I were to cut a slice out of *you*, you creature!"

It spoke in a thick, suety sort of voice, and Alice hadn't a word to say in reply: she could only sit and look at it and gasp.

THROUGH THE LOOKING GLASS

$\frac{1}{2}$ *pint hot milk* | *16 tablespoons dry breadcrumbs* | *8 tablespoons sugar* | *4 well beaten eggs* | $\frac{1}{2}$ *pound shredded suet* | $\frac{1}{2}$ *pound seeded raisins, chopped and floured* | $\frac{1}{4}$ *pound chopped figs* | *2 ounces mixed peel* | *4 tablespoons brandy* | *1 teaspoon grated nutmeg* | *1 teaspoon cinnamon* | $\frac{1}{4}$ *teaspoon mace* | *1$\frac{1}{2}$ teaspoons salt*

1 Soak breadcrumbs in milk in a large mixing bowl.

2 When milk has cooled, add sugar, eggs, raisins, figs and peel.

3 Stir to a creamy consistency.

4 Stir in suet, brandy, nutmeg, cinnamon, mace and salt.

5 The mixture must be stiff, but not dry. Add a little milk only if necessary.

6 Butter a pudding basin.

7 Pack the mixture into the basin until it comes two thirds up the inside—no more or there will be no room for the pudding to expand.

8 Cover top of basin tightly with cooking foil.

9 Place basin in a large saucepan.

10 Add boiling water until it comes half-way up the outside of the basin.

11 Replace saucepan lid.

12 Boil gently for 6 hours, replenishing the water as it boils away.

13 To cool, stand basin in cold water for a few seconds.

14 Either turn out pudding to eat there and then *or* renew the foil and store in a cool place, boiling again for another two hours when you do come to serve it.

15 Serve with custard or cream or very cold rum butter, made by beating together 3 ounces butter, 3 ounces icing sugar and 3 tablespoons of rum in a warm basin.

16 Finally, make sure you don't leave all the conversation to the pudding!

WHAT I LOOK LIKE WHEN I'M LECTURING.
(*From a drawing by Lewis Carroll.*)

Feeding the Mind

Breakfast, dinner, tea; in extreme cases, breakfast, luncheon, dinner, tea, supper, and a glass of something hot at bedtime. What care we take about feeding the lucky body! Which of us does as much for his mind? And what causes the difference? Is the body so much the more important of the two?

By no means: but life depends on the body being fed, whereas we can continue to exist as animals (scarcely as men) though the mind be utterly starved and neglected. Therefore Nature provides that, in case of serious neglect of the body, such terrible consequences of discomfort and pain shall ensue, as will soon bring us back to a sense of our duty: and some of the functions necessary to life she does for us altogether, leaving us no choice in the matter. It would fare but ill with many of us if we were left to superintend our own digestion and circulation. "Bless me!" one would cry, "I forgot to wind up my heart this morning! To think that it has been standing still for the last three hours!" "I can't walk with you this afternoon," a friend would say, "as I have no less than eleven dinners to digest. I had to let them stand over from last week, being so busy, and my doctor says he will not answer for the consequences if I wait any longer!"

Well, it is, I say, for us that the consequences of neglecting the body can be clearly seen and felt; and it might be well for some if the mind were equally visible and tangible—if we could take it, say, to the doctor and have its pulse felt.

"Why, what have you been doing with this mind lately? How have you fed it? It looks pale, and the pulse is very slow."

"Well, doctor, it has not had much regular food lately. I gave it a lot of sugar-plums yesterday."

"Sugar-plums! What kind?"

"Well, they were a parcel of conundrums, sir."

"Ah, I thought so. Now just mind this: if you go on playing tricks like that, you'll spoil all its teeth, and get laid up with mental indigestion. You must have nothing but the plainest reading for the next few days. Take care now! No novels on any account!"

Considering the amount of painful experience many of us have had in feeding and dosing the body, it would, I think, be quite worth our while to try and translate some of the rules into corresponding ones for the mind.

First, then, we should set ourselves to provide for our mind its *proper kind* of food. We very soon learn what will, and what will not, agree with the body, and find little difficulty in refusing a piece of the tempting pudding or pie which is associated in our memory with that terrible attack of indigestion, and whose very name irresistibly recalls rhubarb and magnesia; but it takes a great many lessons to convince us how indigestible some of our favourite lines of reading are, and again and again we make a meal of the unwholesome novel, sure to be followed by its usual train of low spirits, unwillingness to work, weariness of existence—in fact, by mental nightmare.

Then we should be careful to provide this wholesome food in *proper amount*. Mental gluttony, or over-reading, is a dangerous propensity, tending to weakness of digestive power, and in some cases to loss of appetite: we know that bread is a good and wholesome food, but who would like to try the experiment of eating two or three loaves at a sitting?

I have heard a physician telling his patient—whose complaint was merely gluttony and want of exercise—that "the earliest symptom of hyper-nutrition is a deposition of adipose tissue", and no doubt the fine long words greatly consoled the poor man under his increasing load of fat.

I wonder if there is such a thing in nature as a FAT MIND? I really think I have met with one or two: minds which could not keep up with the slowest trot in conversation; could not jump over a logical fence, to save their lives; always got stuck fast in a narrow argument; and, in short, were fit for nothing but to waddle helplessly through the world.

112

Then, again, though the food be wholesome and in proper amount, we know that we must not consume *too many kinds at once*. Take the thirsty a quart of beer, or a quart of cider, or even a quart of cold tea, and he will probably thank you (though not so heartily in the last case!). But what think you his feelings would be if you offered him a tray containing a little mug of beer, a little mug of cider, another of cold tea, one of hot tea, one of coffee, one of cocoa, and corresponding vessels of milk, water, brandy-and-water, and butter-milk? The sum total might be a quart, but would it be the same thing to the haymaker?

Having settled the proper kind, amount, and variety of our mental food, it remains that we should be careful to allow *proper intervals* between meal and meal, and not swallow the food hastily without mastication, so that it may be thoroughly digested; both which rules, for the body, are also applicable at once to the mind.

First, as to the intervals: these are as really necessary as they are for the body, with this difference only, that while the body requires three or four hours' rest before it is ready for another meal, the mind will in many cases do with three or four minutes. I believe that the interval required is much shorter than is generally supposed, and from personal experience, I would recommend anyone, who has to devote several hours together to one subject of thought, to try the effect of such a break, say once an hour, leaving off for five minutes only each time, but taking care to throw the mind absolutely "out of gear" for those five minutes, and to turn it entirely to other subjects. It is astonishing what an amount of impetus and elasticity the mind recovers during those short periods of rest.

And then, as to the mastication of the food, the mental process answering to this is simply *thinking over* what we read. This is a very much greater exertion of mind than the mere passive taking in the contents of our Author. So much greater an exertion is it, that, as Coleridge says, the mind often "angrily refuses" to put itself to such trouble—so much greater, that we are far too apt to neglect it altogether, and go on pouring in fresh food on the top of the undigested masses already lying there, till the unfortunate mind is fairly swamped under the flood. But the greater the exertion the more valuable, we may be sure, is the effect. One hour of steady thinking over a subject (a solitary walk is as good an opportunity for the process as any other) is worth two or three of reading only. And just consider another effect of

113

this thorough digestion of the books we read; I mean the arranging and "ticketing", so to speak, of the subjects in our minds, so that we can readily refer to them when we want them. Sam Slick tells us that he has learnt several languages in his life, but somehow "couldn't keep the parcels sorted' in his mind. And many a mind that hurries through book after book, without waiting to digest or arrange anything, gets into that sort of condition, and the unfortunate owner finds himself far from fit really to support the character all his friends give him.

"A thoroughly well-read man. Just you try him in any subject, now. You can't puzzle him."

You turn to the thoroughly well-read man. You ask him a question, say, in English history (he is understood to have just finished reading Macaulay). He smiles goodnaturedly, tries to look as if he knew all about it, and proceeds to dive into his mind for the answer. Up comes a handful of very promising facts, but on examination they turn out to belong to the wrong century, and are pitched in again. A second haul brings up a fact much more like the real thing, but, unfortunately, along with it comes a tangle of other things—a fact in political economy, a rule in arithmetic, the ages of his brother's children, and a stanza of Gray's "Elegy", and among all these, the fact he wants has got hopelessly twisted up and entangled. Meanwhile, every one is waiting for his reply, and, as the silence is getting more and more awkward, our well-read friend has to stammer out some half-answer at last, not nearly so clear or so satisfactory as an ordinary schoolboy would have given. And all this for want of making up his knowledge into proper bundles and ticketing them.

Do you know the unfortunate victim of ill-judged mental feeding when you see him? Can you doubt him? Look at him drearily wandering round a reading-room, tasting dish after dish—we beg his pardon, book after book—keeping to none. First a mouthful of novel; but no, faugh! he has had nothing but that to eat for the last week, and is quite tired of the taste. Then a slice of science; but you know at once what the result of that will be—ah, of course, much too tough for *his* teeth. And so on through the whole weary round, which he tried (and failed in) yesterday, and will probably try and fail in to-morrow.

Mr. Oliver Wendell Holmes, in his very amusing book, "The Professor at the Breakfast Table", gives the following rule for knowing whether a

114

human being is young or old: "The crucial experiment is this—offer a bulky bun to the suspected individual just ten minutes before dinner. If this is easily accepted and devoured, the fact of youth is established." He tells us that a human being, "if young, will eat anything at any hour of the day or night."

To ascertain the healthiness of the *mental* appetite of a human animal, place in its hands a short, well-written, but not exciting treatise on some popular object—a mental *bun*, in fact. If it is read with eager interest and perfect attention, *and if the reader can answer questions on the subject afterwards*, the mind is in first-rate working order. If it be politely laid down again, or perhaps lounged over for a few minutes, and then, "I can't read this stupid book! Would you hand me the second volume of 'The Mysterious Murder'?" you may be equally sure that there is something wrong in the mental digestion.

If this paper has given you any useful hints on the important subject of reading, and made you see that it is one's duty no less than one's interest to "read, mark, learn, and inwardly digest" the good books that fall in your way, its purpose will be fulfilled.

Hints for Etiquette;
or, Dining Out Made Easy

The following bluprint by Carroll for behaviour at the dinner table was first published in The Comic Times, *a sometime rival of* Punch, *as early as October 13th, 1855, ten years before the publication of* Alice's Adventures in Wonderland *in 1865 and sixteen years before* Through The Looking-Glass *in 1871. He later included it in* Mischmasch, *one of the household magazines which he edited for the amusement of his brothers and sisters as a boy. Nothing appeared more apt to stand as a last word to this book from the man who was its inspiration, a man who combined humour and fastidiousness in most aspects of his daily routine.*

As caterers for the public taste, we can conscientiously recommend this book to all diners-out who are perfectly unacquainted with the usages of society. However we may regret that our author has confined himself to warning rather than advice, we are bound in justice to say that nothing here stated will be found to contradict the habits of the best circles. The following examples exhibit a depth of penetration and a fullness of experience rarely met with:

I

In proceeding to the dining-room, the gentleman gives one arm to the lady he escorts—it is unusual to offer both.

II

The practice of taking soup with the next gentleman but one is now wisely discontinued; but the custom of asking your host his opinion of the weather immediately on the removal of the first course still prevails.

III

To use a fork with your soup, intimating at the same time to your hostess that you are reserving the spoon for the beef-steaks, is a practice wholly exploded.

IV

On meat being placed before you, there is no possible objection to your eating it, if so disposed; still, in all such delicate cases, be guided entirely by the conduct of those around you.

V

It is always allowable to ask for artichoke jelly with your boiled venison; however, there are houses where this is not supplied.

VI

The method of helping roast turkey with two carving-forks is practicable, but deficient in grace.

VII

We do not recommend the practice of eating cheese with a knife and fork in one hand, and a spoon and wine-glass in the other; there is a kind of awkwardness in the action which no amount of practice can entirely dispel.

VIII

As a general rule, do not kick the shins of the opposite gentleman under the table, if personally unacquainted with him; your pleasantry is liable to be misunderstood—a circumstance at all times unpleasant.

IX

Proposing the health of the boy in buttons immediately on the removal of the cloth is a custom springing from regard to his tender years, rather than from a strict adherence to the rules of etiquette.